STOP PEEING IN THE KITTY LITTER!

Humorous and Heartwarming
Parenting Moments

Russ Towne

Russ Towne Publishing
Campbell, CA
www.RussTowne.com
RussTowne@yahoo.com

Editing: Shayla Eaton, CuriouserEditing.com
Cover Design: Joleene Naylor
Interior Layout: Gail Nelson, e-book-design.com
Cover image courtesy of Yelet and Canstockphoto

ISBN 978-0-692804-18-6

Printed in the United States of America

Also Written By Russ Towne

Nonfiction

Reflections from the Heart of a Grateful Man

From the Heart of a Grateful Man

Reflections of a Grateful Man

Slices of Life—An anthology
of the selected nonfiction stories of several writers

Honest, Honey, That's How It Happened

Fiction

Touched—Short stories and flash fiction

Palpable Imaginings—An anthology of fictional short stories
by several writers in various genres.

Poetry

Kaleidoscope

Tickletoe Tree Poetry—Humorous rhyming story poems for
children and those who are young at heart

Heart Whispers—An anthology of the selected works
of over twenty poets

Books for Young Children

The Beach That Love Built

Tickletoe Tree Poetry

A Day in the Shade of a Tickletoe Tree

The Grumpadinkles

Zach and the Toad Who Rode a Bull

Misty Zebracorn

V. G. and Dexter Dufflebee

Ki-Gra's REALLY, REALLY BIG Day!

The Duck Who Flew Upside Down

Clyde and Friends

Clyde and Hoozy Whatzadingle

Clyde and I Help a Hippo to Fly

Rusty Bear and Thomas Too

Clyde and I

Blogs

A Grateful Man (nonfiction uplifting posts): RussTowne.com
A Grateful Man's Poetry: AGratefulMansPoetry.com
Imaginings of a Grateful Man (fictional short stories):
ImaginingsofaGratefulMan.com
Clyde and Friends (about writing children's stories):
ClydeandFriends.com

Acknowledgments

Thank you to my family for so generously providing the experiences that I've attempted to faithfully capture in these stories.

Thank you also to the publishing professionals whose work enhanced this book:

Shayla Eaton for editing,

Joleene Naylor for cover design,

Gail Nelson for book design.

Dedicated with love to My Beloved and our children Ben, Brian, and Stephanie, without whom this book, and the wonderful life I live, would not be possible.

Contents

Stop Peeing in the Kitty Litter!

Younger Son potty trained himself and did so at a remarkably young age. We quickly learned that it wasn't just because he wanted to "pee like Daddy." One day when My Beloved was working in the kitchen, she heard what sounded like water splattering on sand. Puzzled, she followed the sound, which led to the nearest bathroom. There she saw Brian peeing into the kitty litter box next to the toilet.

I'm pretty certain My Beloved never dreamed she'd utter the next words out of her mouth. "Stop peeing in the kitty litter!"

She asked him why he did it, and he said, "I like the sound it makes." Apparently, that rice cereal isn't the only thing that goes snap, crackle, and pop.

It was kind of funny the first time he did it, but it got much less funny when he got caught doing it several more times, and then did it when we had guests.

The Touch

When our children were young, we were fortunate to have the option of being able to have a parent stay at home to raise our children while the other worked outside the home. My Beloved chose to focus her many talents on raising our children, and I'm so glad she did, as they turned out wonderfully. She made a great full-time mom.

For the most part, I enjoyed being a part-time dad, but must admit that I missed much while I was away from my family working. The story I'm about to share is one of those times.

My Beloved was one of those moms who took our kids to many interesting events, places, and activities. One of their favorite places to visit was the San Francisco Zoo.

One day, while at the zoo, My Beloved took our two boys to the gorilla enclosure. A huge window separated the families of humans from those of gorillas. Older Son was about four years old, and Younger Son was a very active one-year-old who was riding in his stroller at the time.

Older Son was in awe of the gorillas and gently placed his little hand on the window, with his flattened palm facing them.

A giant silverback saw the gesture, walked over to the window, and gently placed his huge hand on the other side of the window exactly opposite to Older Son's hand. They would have been touching if not for the window barely separating them. The young tyke wasn't intimidated by the immense size of the powerful creature. As they stood there facing each other, it was like a powerful connection was being made.

My Beloved said it was a magical moment that took her breath away. I feel the magic just writing about it decades later.

Rusty

When I was in the hospital recovering from lung surgery many years ago, a friend gave a teddy bear to me. He knew that I'd long outgrown such gifts, but seeing how miserable, drugged up, and helpless I was, he decided a teddy bear was symbolically appropriate and might just provide some comfort. It did, and I appreciated the gesture.

The bear was rust-colored, so I called it Rusty. It may also have had something to do with the fact that as a little boy, my nickname was Rusty. I was named after the little boy's character in a television show called *The Adventures of Rin Tin Tin,* Rusty B Troop.

Rusty the bear was with me in the hospital and in the long, painful weeks during my recovery at home.

Later, when I married and we began having children, my family learned how Rusty had been with me throughout my illness. When one of us got sick, Rusty was there to help comfort them. It wasn't long before our young children began bringing Rusty to whomever was sick to help them get better.

Rusty is now over thirty-five years old. He has faithfully been there for everyone in my family many times. His presence is comforting, and he is a symbol of our love.

Rusty has been through a lot with us. Over the years, he has become tattered. He is not much to look at anymore, but you should see the appreciative grin on the face of whomever is ill when he is brought in to them.

Our children are now all adults. As they marry and have families of their own, I have no doubt that such a tradition will continue with a stuffed animal for their families.

In the meantime, Rusty is still here, faithfully and lovingly waiting to help comfort any grandchildren who visits.

Treasure Hunt

I collect coins that are in my pockets at the end of each day, and eventually count and roll them. When our children were fairly young, I'd keep the pennies in a big brass, antique-looking container that looked like a large squat goblet with an oversized bowl.

Rather than occasionally count and roll the pennies, My Beloved and I found a fun and educational way to deal with all of them. We asked our three young children if they'd like to go on a treasure hunt, and they all responded enthusiastically. We told them we'd hidden a treasure along with a whole bunch of clues to help them to try to find it. We said we'd give the first clue to them after they agreed to some simple rules:

"Some clues are for Little Sister, some are for Younger Brother, and some are for Older Brother. Whoever the question is for must be given a few minutes to answer the question without help or hints, and after that time, the others can begin giving hints until the clue is found." They all agreed.

The clues were spread throughout our house and front and back yards, and they varied in level of difficulty for each child. In some cases, we tried to include clues to which only one of the children would know the answer. Clues might be along these lines:

Where you found the old bird's nest last month.

Where you keep the leather thing you catch balls with.

Between pages 22 and 23 of Dad's favorite book (or the book that Mom is reading).

Underneath something that gives us light in the living room.

Wrapped around the thing we mash potatoes with.

In the pocket of your favorite shirt.

Wrapped around the handle of something we dig SMALL holes with.

It's red and you get pulled in it.

We then provided a single clue that would lead them to another clue and so on through about twenty clues, and only the last one would lead them to the treasure of the brass container full of pennies.

It was fun for us to come up with the clues and then watch our children work together to answer them all.

The kids loved the game and enjoyed dividing up their bounty when at last they found their treasure.

Don't Smile!

My Beloved and I found that one of the hardest things about disciplining our young children was staying serious when scolding them—especially when every instinct in our bodies and minds wanted to smile or burst out laughing.

And sometimes, even when we couldn't laugh, we did. I know—bad parents!

What made it even worse is when, for example, one of us attempted to keep a straight face while explaining to our child why they shouldn't stick pudding in their sibling's ear, while our dear spouse cracked up with laughter.

We began to make up rules for each other:

"When I'm scolding a child, don't smile, giggle, snicker, laugh, or guffaw, and for goodness' sake, if you are going to do those things please do it in another room, and if you won't do that, please at least stand behind the kid and do it silently so they don't see or hear you doing it!"

In our house, trying to enforce rules with our spouse tended to be more like making suggested guidelines. We are both wired in such a way that a demand or ultimatum is *guaranteed* to produce the exact opposite effect of whatever the original demanded outcome was supposed to be. So we both learned it was *much* better to request or negotiate rather than to make demands.

Anyway, back to disciplining the kids. They started getting wise to our ploy of being serious when they were facing us while their other parent (the one standing behind them) did their best to remain silent while exploding with laughter. The kids started to quickly—and without warning—turn around to try to catch the parent behind them with anything other than a serious face.

Woe to the parent who got caught!

Of course, as soon as the child turned their back on the parent who'd be standing in front of them, the roles would reverse and Ms. Smiley Pants had to be Ms. Serious, and then I could go from being Mr. Serious to Mr. Smiley Pants, or vice versa.

Now that we're grandparents, we get to watch our adult children and their spouses go through the same thing with their children. Unfortunately, they expect us not to smile when our darling grandchildren are being scolded. My Beloved and I manage to comply with such requests.

Well, at least most—err, some of the time . . .

Get Your Stories Straight!

Like nearly all siblings, our sons sometimes got into quarrels. When that occurred, My Beloved and I attempted to unravel how it started so we could create learning lessons as well as determine fair and appropriate consequences for their actions.

Not surprisingly, their versions of what happened sometimes differed greatly. In those situations where it was clear to us that there were no innocent victims and that they'd both broken some rules, rather than try to unravel their stories (which often created more heat than light), we found what we considered to be a fairly elegant solution.

We sent them into a room and told them that they were to stay in there until they got their stories straight and agreed on what had taken place.

Then we closed the door and waited. At first, we sometimes heard continued bickering, and then silence. But usually fairly quickly, negotiations began. They realized the length of time they'd be stuck in the room with each other, and the severity of their other consequences (if any) became completely dependent on working together to create a story that got them both off the hook.

"Well, maybe you weren't trying to hit me with the ball, and I only shoved you a little bit—just kind of playing around, right?"

"Maybe you didn't eat my ice cream bar and I only thought you did, and maybe I got permission from you to eat your cookies and you just kind of forgot that you said it was okay, right?"

Once they got their stories straight, they came out and told their revised story.

It was interesting and humorous to us that no matter how heated the original argument, or how mistreated by the other they felt they had been, by the time they came out of the room they agreed that the situation had mostly been one big misunderstanding or that the terrible wrongs that had been inflicted on each other weren't nearly as bad as they'd originally thought.

Sometimes the stories were said with almost-gritted teeth, and sometimes they had to work through some amazing mental gymnastics to go from their original stories to the ones that they negotiated.

Sure, we knew that we probably weren't getting the whole truth and nothing but the truth, but we figured we probably weren't getting it before either and we'd only been getting their versions of the truth, anyway.

At least with this "get your stories straight" strategy, they had to work together to solve the problem—instead of My Beloved and me.

Earthquake!

Shortly after moving into our current house in 1989, I was shaken out of a deep sleep. Earthquake! And a big one!

I was disoriented from being jerked awake in darkness in a home I hadn't been in for very long. If you've ever been sleeping in an unfamiliar dark room at 3:00 a.m. and were abruptly awakened by a fire alarm, or other similar unexpected noise, you know how disorienting that can be.

I quickly glanced over to make sure My Beloved was okay, up and moving, and then began to hurry toward the bedroom of our two young boys.

Even before I reached the hallway, something seemed terribly wrong. All hell seemed to break loose at once. Everything began shaking even more violently and there was a loud banging and rattling that I didn't recall hearing from prior earthquakes. My adrenaline and fear soared when I looked down the hall into our boys' room and saw orange flickering. A terrifying thought came to me: *FIRE! Oh my God, the boys!*

I yelled to My Beloved, and as I raced down the hall, I kept bouncing into the walls as both they and I were swaying in the darkness. I don't recall ever feeling that panicked.

A huge wave of relief swept over me as I rushed into their room and I realized it wasn't on fire, but only their orange night light that was flickering in the darkness due to the earthquake.

I ran to their beds. Our youngest son was sitting up in his bed afraid—and probably made more so by my obvious alarm. I grabbed and hugged him while looking for our older boy.

To my shock and amazement, he was still sleeping soundly. Not even my yelling, the extra-loud rattling, or the quake itself woke him. (Until recently when he and his wife had their first child, he could blissfully sleep through the ringing of two loud alarm clocks going off simultaneously for so long that someone else in the house had to come in and shut them off. Now, with an infant of his own to protect and care for, even small noises wake him. Welcome to fatherhood!)

The extra-noisy rattling I'd heard turned out to only be a large brass ornamental spittoon with a wood and metal baton-like thing banging around inside as it was jolted around by the quake.

Soon afterward, the quake ended. Our oldest son had slept right through it. My Beloved was able to go back to sleep. Younger Son and I weren't so lucky. Our adrenaline was still pumping way too much to even consider trying to sleep.

So, we watched a slapstick comedy called *The Great Race* on TV. As we sat together, I hugged him closely and reveled in the feelings of relief and gratitude that my precious family was safe. Younger Son and I spent the whole rest of the night together, laughing and enjoying the movie and each other's company.

He is now a married man and the father of three boys, including a pair of twins. To this day, any time that night is mentioned brings knowing smiles to our faces.

Divide and Conquer

Much of what My Beloved and I learned about parenting was taught to us by our children. For example, if they wanted something and the first parent they asked said no, they'd simply go to the other parent and ask again—conveniently leaving out that the other parent had already declined their request.

We quickly learned to ask the children if they had already asked the other parent, and if so, what the answer had been.

Of course, the children learned to go to the weakest link first. Since neither of us wanted to be the bad guy/gal and there were times when we simply didn't want to make a decision or were too tired to do so, we sometimes punted. I'd say, "Go ask your mother." She'd say, "Go ask your father."

After a while, we realized we could be the good guy/gal by saying, "It's okay with me if it's okay with your dad/mom." That usually went over real well with the other parent who was stuck being the bad guy/gal if *no* was the appropriate response from a mature parent.

"No, you can't have cupcakes for breakfast! What was your father thinking?!"

Which was usually quickly followed by, "Russ! What were you thinking saying the kids could have cupcakes for breakfast?"

Kids are such tattletales sometimes!

Whenever I heard her talking to the kids about one of my *brighter* parental decisions, I often tried to make myself scarce and out of earshot. I had the most remarkable selective hearing at such times—not nearly as good as that employed by our children when they were in trouble, but good nonetheless.

And our kids learned that if they were about to suffer the consequences as the result of their poor decisions or behavior—as opposed to mine—they might get off easy if they could get My Beloved and me to argue regarding the appropriate consequences.

We learned the best defense against that strategy was to have talked about the situation in advance and to have agreed in private before approaching the child about the matter. So while our young children were master manipulators, we learned a strategy or two from them as we worked—only partially successfully——to remain firmly in charge.

When they tried to use the divide-and-conquer mentality to win a battle, we closed ranks and kept a united front.

We even found times when we could use divide-and-conquer strategies as parents. If kids were squabbling, we'd divide them. If they were squabbling a lot—and normal consequences weren't working—we'd sometimes each take a child for one-on-one time so that we could enjoy their presence without the terrible Sibling-Squabble-Monster rearing its ugly head.

As I said, we learned much from our children—probably a lot more than they would have liked.

Parenting "Fun" with Younger Son

My Beloved and I are very proud of all three of our now-grown children. Each of them is unique and special in their own ways. But there were many times when pride wasn't the primary emotion we felt when dealing with them.

This is about Younger Son when he was a child and before he became a husband, physicist, and captain in the USAF.

Way back then he was a:

Fearless Daredevil: I once caught a glimpse of him as he began to fall head-first out of a two story window that was directly above a concrete sidewalk. I have never moved so quickly as I lunged through his bedroom and grabbed his ankles just as they moved through the window. He had stacked stuff under the window so he could reach the ledge.

Fearless Daredevil Part 2: One of Younger Son's favorite pastimes in his early years was throwing himself down a flight of stairs. He liked how he bounced and rolled. Surprisingly, he never broke a bone.

Contortionist: He once managed to squeeze his head between the railings of our staircase into a space that was so tight that we spent an hour trying to get him out. I don't remember everything we tried, but I do remember salad oil and liquid dishwashing soap. What a mess! I was about ready to use a saw or call the fire department when we were finally able to get his head out. I believe it was the dishwashing soap that finally did the trick.

Announcer: Once when My Beloved was in a crowded grocery store, he loudly exclaimed: "I have a penis, huh, Mommy?" She quietly replied yes while trying to get him to turn down the volume several notches. He continued as loud as ever, "You don't have a penis, do you, Mommy?"

Double Trouble: He and his best friend met in kindergarten. They were inseparable, which meant that when they got into trouble, they did it together.

Miner: He and Best Friend decided to dig a hole one day and worked on it for hours. They had gone down three or four feet when My Beloved decided that was deep enough. She told them it was time to fill in the hole. Later, she was impressed at how well they'd filled it in—that is until she walked onto the spot where the hole had been and the ground beneath her feet began bouncing. The little stinkers had put plywood over the hole and covered it with a thin layer of dirt so they could keep working on the hole later. They learned to regret that decision.

Construction Worker: One day Younger Son and Best Friend built a fort out of wood. It was built remarkably well for two young boys and was quite sturdy. We were proud of what they had accomplished—right up until My Beloved heard Little

Sister yelling and found they had decided it would be fun to have her go into the fort and then nail the door shut! That stunt cost them their fort and a few other consequences.

Hallway Torture

One of the toughest challenges My Beloved and I had as parents was regarding discipline. We wanted to be firm but loving and fair, and for the consequences to be effective, age-appropriate, and child-specific.

Unfortunately, it quickly became obvious that what is a behavior-changing consequence for one child could be a nice break from routine for another.

Just about the time we found a consequence that worked for one child, it tended to quickly stop working for another—even when it had been working very well only a week earlier.

We also quickly learned that longer-term consequences such as "If you do that, you will be grounded for a month" not only rarely deterred the behavior that we sought to avoid, but it also seemed to be more punishment for us to attempt to consistently enforce it than it was an effective consequence for them.

We strongly preferred consequences that were quickly dealt and then done, so they—and we—could get on with life. But such consequences that were also consistently effective were rare indeed.

We tried all sorts of things, and most weren't effective deterrents for long. That became especially true as they got older.

That is, until we discovered Hallway Torture—err, I mean,

Hallway Time. Our kids absolutely *hated* being bored. And there is nothing to do, play with, or read in our hallway. We found that if we told one of our children to sit in the hallway for a certain number of minutes as a consequence that it was often a very effective deterrent.

That doesn't mean that they didn't constantly try to see what they could get away with in the hallway. They tried reading books or bringing in toys or games.

Rule change: No books, games, or toys (and if our children weren't already grown-up adults and if we were parenting children today, we'd definitely also prohibit all electronic devices).

They tried hounding us with questions such as, "Is the time over yet?"

Rule Change: No talking. If you talk, extra Hallway Time is added. (That backfired on us once when we forgot and a child was left in the hallway for much longer than they were supposed to. I don't recall what we did to make it up to that poor kid, but I know it left them with a big smile!)

They tried sleeping.

Rule change: No sleeping. If you sleep, extra time is added. If you have to, stand up so you don't fall asleep. This isn't nap or reward time; it's consequence time.

We even found it worked for twofers. When two of our children got into trouble together (especially if it was from bickering with each other), Hallway Time often worked perfectly to change the behavior.

Of course, they would try to bend the rules by whispering to each other, but we'd learned a few things by then too.

New rules included: Be at opposite ends of the hallway; no talking, singing, or whispering; no touching/pushing/shoving or body contact of any kind. No giggling or laughing. (They would sometimes make funny faces or do silly things to try to get the other to laugh out loud and get into trouble.)

All infractions meant—you guessed it—more hallway time.

We have an L-shaped hallway. To make it easier on our children to comply with the rules—and on us in enforcing them—we often placed the kids at opposite ends of the hallway and around the corner from each other.

Hallway Time proved to be the most effective and longest-lasting consequence for all three of our children that we ever came up with.

Your mileage may vary.

How a Daunting Gauntlet Became a Fun Zone

Some years ago, I was standing in a long, long line at a major theme park in southern California with My Beloved and our children. I was bored, hot, and tired. I stuck a hand in my pocket and noticed that a sizable pile of coins had built up from all the change I'd received from the various park vendors.

An idea came to me that made my whole experience so much more pleasant and even fun. I took out a quarter, and when no one was looking, I tossed it onto the ground near the sidewalk on which we were standing, very close to one of our children. The soil softened the sound of the coin falling. The quarter shined brightly in the summer sun and sure enough, one child saw and picked it up, excitedly exclaiming to us parents: "Look what i found!" He beamed from ear to ear. I smiled just as big on the inside.

I whispered what I'd done to My Beloved so she could enjoy the experience too. I tossed a few more coins and got similar excited reactions from our other children, and then began to do the same for children from other families.

The serpentine line crawled along ever so slowly, and we eventually got to the point where pavement was all around us, and the noise of coins hitting the hard surface would soon give me away.

I experimented and found that I could drop a coin onto the top of my shoes and the coin would roll off quietly, partially muffled by the murmuring crowd. I waited until several young children were on both sides of us in the twisting line and as carefully and quietly as I could, I began sending coins their way. It was great to watch the children as they found and showed off their prize to their parents.

We smiled at each other. Soon, other parents started catching me as I released the coins. They gave knowing looks to me, grinned, and didn't say a thing. One winked. It became even more fun as other parents shared our little secret. They played their part by acting surprised at the treasure that the children discovered.

If a child didn't see a coin near them, sometimes a parent would point at it and say to their youngster, "Oh, look, what's that?" That's all it took to start the joyful reaction.

That simple idea was so much fun and cost so little that it was one of the best entertainment values I've ever had!

Now, long lines full of young children are opportunities rather than the daunting gauntlets they sometimes used to appear to be. They are opportunities to bring joy and smiles to young children, their parents, My Beloved, and me.

Sock War

One day when our boys were still fairly young, I kidded My Beloved about something as she sorted and matched a basket of clean socks, rolling the matched pairs into little balls to keep them together. The next thing I knew, a pair of rolled-up socks was flying at me at roughly the speed of sound and hit me squarely between the eyes!

My Beloved had an amazingly accurate throwing arm, and she knew how to use it. She had signed with a pro women's softball league right out of high school after being voted the most athletic girl in our school. So, when I say My Beloved could throw like a pro, I'm not exaggerating.

Luckily for me, a pair of rolled-up cotton socks has not much greater of an impact than a cotton ball.

"Two can play that game," I yelled as I ran over and grabbed a bunch of the sock balls from her pile, and then ran behind a couch and lobbed a pair at her. She ducked behind a chair with a handful of her own, and the Sock War was on!

By now, our young boys were laughing hysterically. They grabbed some sock balls and ducked behind other furniture as the Sock War escalated. Sock balls were flying everywhere and bouncing off of everyone and everything! We were all laughing so hard our eyes began watering.

A cool thing about Sock Wars (besides that no one in our family ever got hurt fighting them) is no one ever runs out of ammunition.

We played until our arms couldn't throw anymore and laughed so long and hard our jaws ached.

Sock Wars became one of our favorite family traditions, and we often played it.

The game's only rule was that you couldn't throw dirty socks. Considering how smelly the boys and my feet were, you can probably guess who invented that rule.

Braces

Sometimes it is really tough to be a kid. When both of our boys needed braces, we knew they were in for a rough time. In those days, braces tended to be made out of highly visible shiny metal and were very painful. We also knew that some kids would make fun of their "railroad tracks" and that could be hard on their self-esteem.

From the perspective of our sons, there was yet another big negative. The dentist gave them a long list of chewy, gooey, wonderful things they could *not* eat for the entire time they had to wear the braces, and they were warned that if they did eat the banned items, they could cause permanent damage to their teeth and expensive damage to their braces.

The looks on their faces fell and stayed that way as the time for braces neared.

It hurt My Beloved and me to see them so sad, so we discussed the situation. We agreed that there wasn't much we could do about the emotional and physical pain, nor the taunting they were likely to get at school, beyond our being open to discussing such things at whatever level the boys might feel comfortable in doing so. We didn't want to baby them, and we wanted to support them in a healthy way.

We were also concerned that they might have a very hard

time refraining from all of the goodies that were on the dentist's banned list, so we came up with an idea that we thought might at least remove some of the sting of getting braces.

A week or two before they were scheduled to get their braces, My Beloved and I sat them down and said we knew it would be tough to keep from eating all the things that were on the banned list for the whole time they wore their braces, so we were willing to make a deal with them.

We'd take them to the grocery store and let them each cram as many of their favorite items from the banned list as they could into their own large lunch bag, and then we'd let them eat it all.

We told them we expected four things in return. That they would:

Continue to eat three healthy meals per day,

Thoroughly brush their teeth a minimum of three times every day,

Finish eating everything in the bag or hand over any that they hadn't eaten before the braces were put on, and

They wouldn't eat any of the items on the banned list for the whole time their braces were on.

Their faces lit up as they enthusiastically agreed to the terms of our agreement, so we jumped into the car and went to the grocery store with their two empty bags.

Talk about kids in a candy store! They quickly filled their bags with all kinds of wonderful stuff, carefully using every millimeter of space as they scientifically jammed more of their treasure into their bulging bags.

When we got home, they were thrilled with all of their goodies and began to enjoy their bounty. They were so happy that I think they even forgot about the braces for a while.

We ensured that they had healthy meals and brushed their teeth often, but otherwise left them to their goodies.

As we'd hoped, by the time their braces went on, the boys were so sick of all that junk that quite a long time elapsed before they even wanted to *think* about eating anything on the banned list again!

A Rite of Passage

My Beloved spent many of her formative years on a farm and knew what it was like to work hard.

As a city boy, I didn't know as much about working hard, but I did chop firewood for my grandparents in Oregon when my family visited from California. They needed a lot of it, as it was the only source of heat for their house and winters got very cold in that part of the state.

And as the oldest of five children, when both my parents went to work to support us, my next-oldest sister and I ended up taking on a sizable number of chores to keep the household running. We felt like we had the whole weight of the house on our shoulders. It was far from the truth, but that is what my sister and I had thought at the time.

When My Beloved and I became adults with young kids of our own, we were concerned that because we lived in a suburb of a large city with a stay-at-home mother, they might never truly have much opportunity to do hard physical labor or to see how much they could accomplish physically. We wanted our children to have the opportunity to work hard and to feel good about themselves when they did.

My Beloved and I came up with an idea. We lived on a quarter-acre property and had three lawns of varying sizes that needed mowing. We had an old-fashioned human-powered push mower, and when I judged that each child was at about the right size, it became their responsibility to mow the lawns. "About the right size" was when the child would have to reach up to grab the handle and had to lean into the monster with all their might to get it moving.

When I presented the *opportunity* to each child as they reached about the right size, they were far less than enthusiastic. They gave their best "You've *got* to be kidding, Dad!" look to me and frowned. Their frowns didn't last long, though. No, they became scowls instead when they learned that there was a job they had to do before they could mow the lawn. We have dogs, and like any well-behaved, self-respecting dogs, they do their business outside. On our lawns.

So I handed a pooper-scooper and bag to them along with some sage fatherly advice:

"It would be a very good idea to be sure to pick up all the mess first, because your situation will be much worse if you begin mowing the lawn when it isn't."

They didn't need to be told twice. Once they were done with that "fun" job, the real work began. I showed them how to safely use a push mower, and then let them give it a try. They grabbed the handle with both hands and pushed. Nothing. They pushed harder. The mower began to lean in the right direction but still didn't move. Then they pushed with all their might and the mower slowly moved forward.

I watched them for a while, coaching and cheering them

on, and then went inside while keeping an eye on them from a window. I wanted them to be able to do it all by themselves and to know that they'd done it without help. The job took all they had, but they gave it their all. I can still see the proud and exhausted looks on their faces when they finished it.

The job grew easier as they grew and developed greater physical strength. About the time it became too easy for Older Son, Younger Son was about the right size. I took him outside, pointed to the mower, and he gave me his best "You've got to be kidding, Dad!" look and frowned.

As I began to mention the job that needed to be done before he could begin mowing, I noticed out of the corner of my eye a big grin and a knowing look on Older Son's face.

A Lesson I Learned from My Son and Dandelions

When Younger Son was in his early teens, one of his chores was to mow the lawn. One day as I walked into the house after work, I noticed that the front yard had a lot of dandelion stems in it that were at least six inches tall. On top of them were the round puff balls that blew apart on windy days. My son had promised to mow the yard the day before, but looking at those tall dandelions, it was clear to me he hadn't done so.

When I asked him if he'd mowed the lawn, he said he had. I then asked if he'd done a good job, and received the same answer. I began getting angry.

I asked him how he could possibly have mowed the yard the day before when the dandelions were so tall today? He swore to me that he had indeed mowed the yard the day before.

I was convinced he was lying, and children who got caught doing that in our house faced substantial consequences—often extra yard work.

My wife and I preferred to give yard work as a consequence because it could be quickly completed and wasn't easy. That way, the lesson we were trying to instill would more likely be learned and remembered.

I was about to assign a consequence to my son for lying to me, but something kept me from doing it. Perhaps it was because he didn't tend to lie. Maybe it was the earnest look in his eyes, or that he was so adamant about his innocence. Whatever the reason, I decided on a simple way to prove the truth.

I asked him to mow the yard again the next day just before I came home from work. Then when I got home, I'd ensure the job was done well. The following day, we'd both take a look at the lawn and if I didn't see tall dandelions with the puff balls on top, I'd know he'd lied to me.

I warned him that if the experiment proved that he were lying, the consequence would be even worse for him than if he admitted it right then. Once again, he said he was telling the truth.

After work the next day, I checked the lawn and he had indeed thoroughly mowed it. There wasn't a dandelion puff ball or tall stem in sight.

When I came home from work the following day, I looked at the front yard. To my shock and amazement, there were many dandelion stems standing six inches tall. In just one day, they had grown that high and sprouted puff balls!

There was now no doubt that he had been telling the truth. I felt shame for having accused him of lying to me. I asked him to come out to the front yard, and I sincerely apologized for falsely accusing him. I added that there be no consequence to him, and that we'd do something special so that I could help make it up to him for my not trusting him when he'd given his word that he'd mowed the lawn.

My son and those dandelions taught me some important lessons that day:

I should have trusted him as I usually do.

Never underestimate either my son or nature; both can do amazing things.

Sometimes my eyes can deceive me, and it is good to ask my heart for a second opinion.

The Beach That Love Built

When our daughter was about fifteen, she was stricken with an incurable disease and nearly died. She spent about a month in the hospital, much of it in intensive care fighting for her life. She had to deal with an awful disease as well as many blood transfusions and the side effects of the chemotherapy, steroids, and other harsh medications. She met each challenge, disappointment, and setback with courage and class.

Eventually, the disease went into remission and she began to dream of having a party and bonfire for her sixteenth birthday at the beach with her friends, relatives, and beloved dog Ginger. It took quite a bit of searching, but we finally found a beach that had all the necessary attributes, including allowing dogs and bonfires, and that had easy to access for elderly relatives.

A week before her party, the disease flared up and fifteen glorious months of remission ended.

Then, at 9:00 p.m., the night before the party, a friend called with some news that turned our plans upside down. He'd just heard that the small beach we'd selected and the surrounding beaches were about to be overwhelmed by a 30,000-person event that would make them unusable for our planned party.

No other beach within a reasonable driving distance had all of the attributes required to make her dream come true.

Our daughter had her heart set on having her family and friends, dog, and a bonfire at the beach, but as usual, she didn't complain. In her young life, she has had to deal with much worse things than a spoiled birthday party. But it was just the final straw on a mountain of straws that finally broke the camel's back. She sat down and quietly began to cry.

She then quickly decided that she'd rather have the party at our home so that she could at least have her dog, relatives, friends, and a bonfire. We began making the calls to invitees about the changed plans.

The next day when guests began arriving at our home (which is about thirty miles from the nearest beach), they were surprised to find a sign that read:

"Welcome to our beach, where the waves are so far away you need to close your eyes to see them, but not the love for our daughter and her little dog too. Dogs and bonfires are welcome! Happy Birthday!"

Laid out before them was the smallest, goofiest beach they'd ever seen, but it had been built with love. Our friends had at a moment's notice dreamt up creating a beach in our backyard. They had surprised us several hours earlier with a car loaded down with 660 pounds of sand, a palm tree, beach toys, fish netting, tiki torches, and much more. Our friends and son helped set up everything.

The beach was built with so much love that it quickly became real to everyone there. The birthday girl and her friends frolicked in the sand, had a barbecue, built their own huge ice-cream sundaes, and splashed in the water of a little pool. Then as night fell, they lit the tiki torches and enjoyed a great bonfire.

In the darkness, by the light of the torches and bonfire, and with the joyous splashing sounds and giggling from those playing in the water of the small wading pool in the background, the scene had indeed seemed to magically transform into a beach.

That night as the girls laughed and played on the "beach" around the bonfire with our funny little dog, I felt for a moment that all was right in the world, and was very grateful to our friends for making our daughter's birthday wish come true after all.

A Most Unusual Christmas Tree

The sight of a most unusual Christmas tree often greets visitors to our home near the holidays. Instead of a fir or some other traditional kind, we have a *palm* tree. It is decorated with Christmas lights and ornaments, and is topped by a strange-looking star made of cardboard covered by several layers of aluminum foil and tape. All five of the star's points are somewhat different in shape, size, and angle.

That tree and star have a very special place in my heart, and each has a story.

The palm tree is the same one just featured in my last story that helped to create such a special time for those at our Beach That Love Built.

A couple of months later, as the holidays neared, our daughter suggested that we use the palm tree that helped make the "beach" so special instead of getting a Christmas tree. We liked the idea so much that it is now the tree we've used most years ever since.

The story of the star that sits atop the tree goes back almost forty years. I was a young single man whose business was failing. Finances were very tight. I had enough money to buy a Christmas tree but not enough for ornaments or other decorations. A young woman I was dating at the time saw how bare the tree looked. She made a big star out of a piece of cardboard she'd cut out herself and then wrapped in aluminum foil she taped to it. It sure looked good on top of my nearly bare tree! A year later, that young woman be came my wife.

That star has sat in the place of honor on our Christmas trees ever since. During all the good years, it reminds us of times when things weren't so good, and during rough years, it reminds us that bad times don't last forever. But most of all, it reminds us as to how blessed we are to have the love of our family and friends.

Over the years, the star became ragged-looking and has often been repaired by adding more aluminum foil and tape. My wife sometimes suggests that we replace it with a store-bought treetop ornament, but I can't bring myself to do it, because that star—and now that most unusual Christmas tree that so proudly holds it up—is a powerful reminder of the wonderful acts of love that embody the true Spirit of Christmas.

A War of Wills

As parents, My Beloved and I were blessed with remarkably honest children. So honest, in fact, that they were downright lousy liars due to lack of practice. That often made it relatively easy for us to quickly learn the truth even during the rare times they crossed that line.

Once, when Older Son was perhaps ten or twelve years old, he took a piece of gum that wasn't his. We taught our children that if someone takes something that isn't theirs without first getting permission, it is stealing, and stealing is a serious matter that always has consequences.

It was only a piece of gum, and Oldest Son knew if he quickly admitted to taking the gum, he would probably just get a reprimand and be asked to buy a pack of gum for the family member from whom he took it. Instead of telling the truth, he denied taking it. It was obvious by his facial expressions and body language that he was lying.

My Beloved and I taught our children from an early age that if they broke the rules, there would be consequences, but if they lied about breaking the rules, the consequences would be *far* worse than if they had told the truth right away. We then made certain the consequences for lying were indeed *much* worse than they would have been for telling the truth about breaking the rule.

Older Son knew all of this and still denied taking the gum, even after being reminded about what happens when someone lies in our house. He was normally a well-behaved child but this time chose a different path. He dug in his heels and refused to admit he took the gum. An extra chore was assigned to him. It was unpleasant but could have been done in about an hour.

When I returned home from work the next day, Older Son still refused to admit he'd taken the gum, *and* he hadn't done the extra chore. He was clearly exercising his independence. Such moments are not what I think of when the phrase "The joys of parenting" comes to mind.

It was time to escalate the consequence. I reminded him that this all started over a single piece of gum, and now he had two hours worth of yard work to do before I came home from work the next day.

The following evening, he neither confessed nor had done the yard work. I knew this was a war of wills that for the sake of both of us I had to win as a parent. I led him outside to a large section of what had once been a garden that was now filled with weeds. I told him I expected a large section of it to be free of weeds by the next day.

The following evening, very little weeding had been done. I was seething. I knew that a big event in which he badly wanted to participate was coming up soon and I gave an ultimatum to him:

"Weed the *entire* area (a space of about fifteen feet by fifty feet) this weekend." It was Friday evening. I added for good measure, "You have until midnight Sunday to finish the job, and I don't care if you have to be out here weeding by flashlight. There better not be so much as a single blade of grass in this whole area, or you won't be going to (whatever the important function was)."

Finally, that got his attention. He got up about mid-morning on Saturday and began working. He worked slowly but somewhat diligently. Unfortunately, when he dragged himself in on Saturday night at about dark, he was only about one-quarter done with what had become a big job.

I began to feel sorry for him, but he knew I wouldn't break my promise as to what would happen to him if he didn't meet the deadline. Breaking my word wouldn't be good for him and would just make it harder for both of us the next time we had a war of wills. He needed to be able to count on my word and me.

He began working quite early Sunday morning. His pace was much faster than the day before. He was clearly on a mission. He worked hard for many hours and had made good progress, but as dusk approached, he was nowhere near done.

He kept working even as it became too dark to see him through the window. Then I saw the beam of a flashlight. I occasionally looked out the window and watched the beam continue moving as he worked. Hours later, right at midnight, he came in covered in dirt and sweat. With an exhausted voice, he said, "I'm done."

"Did you get every weed and blade of grass?"

He nodded yes.

"Okay, get some rest. We'll look at it in the morning."

Early the next day, as we went out to see the job he'd done, I mentally prepared myself for seeing some missed small weeds and blades of grass. I decided that if he did as good a job as one could expect for a boy his age, I would cut him some slack for the tremendous effort he'd made.

I'll never forget what I saw. The large space that had been completely covered in weeds two days before did not have a single weed or blade of grass anywhere on it. I gaped in awe and amazement, knowing that if I'd been given the task, I wouldn't have done nearly the perfect job he'd done.

I saw the pride in his eyes at the job he'd done. I hope he saw the same in mine when I looked at him and said, "I'm proud of you for the job you did."

No truer words were ever spoken.

Oops!

One day, when Older Son was learning to drive, My Beloved went with him when he was behind the wheel to let him practice and to provide lessons and coaching along the way.

As usual, he did quite well despite having to deal with relatively heavy urban and suburban traffic. Then the trouble started.

He didn't see a stop sign and blew right through it. Fortunately, no cars were coming. My Beloved quickly pointed out to him what he'd done.

There are many ways that Older Son could have reacted, and many things he could have said. Unfortunately for him, what he chose to do and say weren't among the better choices.

He shrugged, smiled, and said, "Oops!"

He might as well have thrown raw meat to a hungry tigress.

I'll spare you the gory details, but suffice it to say, it was the end of his lesson that day, and the end of any driving practice for quite a while afterward. He never reacted that way to a driving mistake again.

Prom Nightmare

Older Son had a very "memorable" prom night. "Memorable" as in, "Is this terrible night ever going to end?"

It had started well enough. Although he had a vehicle of his own, I'd offered to lend him my brand-spanking-new *gorgeous* car of my dreams that I'd been pining over for a long time and had finally bought. So, to say I loved this car would be an understatement—and there are very few material things love. When I handed my keys to him, he knew how much faith I had in him.

He was all decked out in his impressive Jr. ROTC USMC dress blues uniform, and had a corsage for his lovely date. As he backed out of our driveway on his way to pick her up, I mentally checked off two more rites of passage for each of us:

1. Older Son going to his high school prom.
2. Older Son driving my new car for the first time.

He was proud and nervous. So was his dad.

When he got to the home where his date lived, there was a long, narrow driveway that was squeezed between a long fence and her parents' home.

He parked and greeted her parents in the time-honored ritual that is dreaded by both the young man and the young girl's father. I have no idea what it feels like to be the young girl or her mom, but I *know* how it is for the young man and father and let's just say it isn't high on my favorite things to do.

After everyone survived that awkward ordeal, he opened the car door for his date—he was well trained—then got in on the driver's side, and they waved goodbye to her parents.

He'd made a mental note to himself about how close he was to their house so he carefully avoided the house as he backed out. Thankfully, he didn't hit their house.

He hit their fence instead. And not just a few feet of it. A *lot* of it.

He was unfamiliar with the accelerator and raced backward quite a bit faster than he planned, turning much of their fence into splintered firewood. In front of her parents. And he did it not by jamming my bumper into the fence. That would have only created minor damage to my car. No, he used the whole back half of the driver's side of my car to do it. (It's funny as I typed this, I thought of the *Titanic*. It hit the iceberg at the worst possible angle and then dragged along much of its side, doing major damage along a large length of it. That's exactly what Older Son had managed to do.) His thoughts for a happy and fun prom night sank even faster than that ill-fated ship.

He got out, surveyed the damage, and couldn't believe how extensive it was—-to the fence and to the car. He apologized profusely to his date's parents. They were remarkably kind to him and good-natured about the whole thing. He offered to pay for the damage to their fence, and then got back in what was left of my car and headed for the prom.

On a major freeway, one of the brand-new, high-performance, driver's-side tires blew out. He had probably picked up a nail from the fence collision and it had taken awhile to penetrate far enough into the tire to cause the blowout. He got the car off the freeway and changed the tire in his fancy dress uniform. The spare was one of those little temporary tires that looks ridiculous on a car.

He finally got them safely to the prom, but I've got to believe that he was so concerned about how I would react to all the damage that I doubt he had a very good time.

When the prom was over, he was able to get his date home safely—a minor miracle by itself considering what had gone wrong that night. It was late when he came home. He probably hoped I was asleep.

I wasn't.

I looked out the kitchen window when he drove up. What I saw was a car that looked like it had been in a *major* wreck. As he got out of the car, I was relieved to see he appeared unhurt. I noticed that my first and final reactions were exactly the same: *He's okay, she's okay* (I knew this instinctively because he'd have called me right away if anyone had gotten hurt), and *it's only a car.*

I have to say that I was a little surprised by the latter. And relieved. And happy. And proud. It was, after all, only a car. I knew then that I still had my priorities straight, and it felt good.

I think he came in steeled for the worst, and what he got

was a relieved parent who calmly heard his story and said, "Don't worry about it. We'll deal with it tomorrow. Let's get some sleep."

Bathroom Battles

The five of us lived in a little home with a single bathroom in the house. It was tough enough when the children were little, and many times worse when all the children were teenagers and wanted their own private time in the bathroom. A key rule was no one could be in there by themselves unless they were actually using the toilet, shower, or bathtub.

After long car trips, I think we broke speed records as we raced to get to the bathroom first.

Often our work and school schedules collided and the collisions invariably occurred in our tiny, one-sink bathroom. There were times when three or four of us would all be trying to use the sink, mirror, and counter at the same time. Add impatience, school bells, bosses, sibling rivalry, and morning grogginess to the mix and noisy chaos reigned. It was like we were all playing a raucous vertical game of Twister.

Battles were fought over every square inch of that tiny room. Elbows flew, complaints were voiced, and bodies pushed and squeezed. It was dangerous trying to shave, brush teeth, put on makeup, brush and comb hair, and the like, in such a jarring environement.

Thankfully, over time, for self-preservation and efficiency, we gradually became so synchronized in fast motion that we probably could have won a contest.

Clasped Hands

On a shelf near my desk are a couple of chunks of something that I value more than if they were made of solid gold or chiseled by a master sculptor out of the finest marble.

They were made at weekend events called Fathers, Sons, and Brothers that were created to celebrate the love of strong male relationships and to honor each other in them, as well as to help those who grieved the loss of a father, son, or brother, or were in pain from damaged, broken, or nonexistent relationships.

I went with my dad for one of the events, Older Son for the second, and Younger Son for the third—-the latter two when they were young adults. Each weekend was a powerful celebration that also included forgiveness and healing. They reinforced to me, my father, and my two sons just how blessed we were to all be alive, healthy, and in strong, loving relationships with each other.

During the second and third such weekends, a man introduced a process that was quite remarkable in its simplicity and quite powerful in its result.

He asked each father and son to sit at a picnic table across from each other and to clasp each other's right hand as though we were going to arm wrestle, but leaving our hands upright, and then to hold that position until he said to let go. He then began to put some cloth mesh all over our hands and then slathered a thick layer of that paper mache goop over the mesh covering our hands. He then reminded us not to move, and then went to the next father-son pair to begin the process again.

At first, it was a bit awkward. We were leaning toward each other with our faces only two to three feet apart and with our hands covered by a big glob of white goop—a bit out of the ordinary to say the least. After a while, we relaxed and just started talking to each other. We were closer longer physically to each other than perhaps at any time since my boys were infants or young children. It was intimate, and it was special. We enjoyed the time together.

When the goop on our hands solidified, the man very carefully cracked it off to keep the mold that he created intact. As we washed our hands, he poured new paper mache goop into the mold we'd just made. When the goop dried, he broke apart the mold to reveal a life-sized and remarkably accurate replica of us clasping hands. Every finger, knuckle, and nail was visible.

We looked at it and knew that it was a symbol of the strength of our love and our bond, and the respect we have for each other. I value those hunks of paper mache more than if they were made of solid gold or chiseled by a master sculptor out of the finest marble. I see them several times per day and they often bring a smile to my face.

When my time on this planet is done, my sons will each get the one with their hand and mine.

And eventually, perhaps their children will get them too.

Send in the Cavalry!

As our children got into their mid- to later-teen years, they and their friends used to hang out a lot at our house, and usually in our living room. It probably had a lot to do with the fact that My Beloved is a good cook and always made way too much food for our family, so our kids' friends were often invited to dinner or to enjoy the leftovers.

I like to believe that it also had something to do with the fact that they felt safe and welcome in our home, and they thought that we were reasonably cool or okay parents and adults—or at least that we were a little less un-cool and weird than their other options.

We mostly loved that they spent so much time at our house. All of them were good kids, and we knew where they were and what they were up to most of the time.

Sometimes, however, a good thing can become too much. Since they weren't old enough to go to bars, and they felt they were too old to do things like bowling or miniature golf, their options for what to do fairly late at night became very limited.

Often, way too often, My Beloved and I heard this conversation for most of the evening:

"What do you want to do tonight?"

"I don't know. What do you want to do?"

(Repeat ad nauseam.)

They'd keep up that "conversation" for so long that it would be too late to do anything except go to a twenty-four-hour restaurant, the *same* restaurant they'd been to every night for what seemed like months.

One night, when the monotonous conversation began, I'd had enough and wanted to reclaim my living room from the hungry horde of bored teenagers earlier than 11:00 p.m.

Without saying a word, I got up and picked out a cavalry movie—I loved cavalry movies—and stuck it in the movie player. The next thing those teenagers heard was the sound of a bugler blowing *CHARGE!*

I've never seen so many teenagers clear out so fast!

Apparently, they weren't fond of cavalry movies.

After that, whenever I wanted my living room back, all I had to do is ask out loud, "Now where'd I put that cavalry movie?"

Dads and Daughters

I work from home. We live in an old, rural-looking neighborhood where all of the mailboxes for houses on both sides of the street are on the side that is across the street from our house. Near the mailboxes, a house was being built.

When I went to put out the mail that morning, I noticed a car parked in front of my house with a young girl perhaps eight to ten years of age sitting in the backseat. I smiled to her when I walked back toward my house and got a beautiful, friendly smile in return. Her face lit up.

She appeared to be the daughter of one of the day workers and was most likely out of school for Columbus Day. She was clearly in no danger, as her father was keeping an attentive eye on her from across the street, and the weather was beautiful. The windows were open and the temperatures were perfect so that there was no chance of her being in a car that would heat up inside to anywhere near unsafe levels.

But I felt bad for the daughter and for her father. He probably felt she was too young to stay home alone, and the construction site was way too dangerous for her to be across the street with him. So, he appeared to have done the best he could for her in a bad situation.

If I were a woman, I'd have talked to the father and invited the girl to play in our yard, perhaps even with our dogs if he approved, and if she liked.

But I am not a woman. I am a man and a father of a girl, and if I were that man and my daughter were the one in the car at that young age, I would be very concerned about a strange man being in any way attentive to her. And there is no way I'd want the man asking if my daughter could play in his yard.

But seeing that girl sitting alone in that car all morning—and who would probably be there all day—saddened me. I wanted to find some way to help relieve her boredom, to cheer her up, and to let her know that she is important, and that other people care for her well-being.

It occurred to me that my daughter (who at that point was a young adult) was home and that we had a frosty bottle of root beer in our fridge. I asked her if she'd be willing to take it out to the girl and offer it to her while it was still unopened—that way, the father and the girl could be assured that its contents hadn't been tampered with. I suggested she bring a bottle opener and if the girl accepted the root beer, to please open it for her so the dad could see what was going on.

My daughter agreed, and the girl accepted the soda. As this was going on, I noticed that the girl's father, while still continuing to work, moved to the edge of the construction site nearest his daughter and watched without appearing to do so. It pleased me greatly to see how much he cared for his daughter and how carefully he protected her.

I was also happy that a dad and his daughter were able to find a way to show kindness to a daughter in front of her dad in a non-threatening way.

A Bad Day at the "Office"

One night when Daughter was in her early twenties, she came home from her park ranger intern job looking physically and emotionally drained. She came up and hugged me for a long time. I hadn't had a "I need a hug, Daddy, please comfort me and make the world go away" hug like that in a long time. I loved it, but was of course immediately concerned.

While I gave her my best "Daddy is here, you're safe, and it will all be okay" hug, my concern turned to alarm at the thought that perhaps she was having a severe relapse of her medical condition. Flashes of blood transfusions, long stays in the intensive care unit, and worse started going off in my head.

I was greatly relieved when she said, while still tightly hugging me, that she and her ranger mentor had responded to a horrible car accident involving four seventeen-year-olds. One victim was so badly hurt that she had to firmly hold his head to avoid further possible spinal damage while they lifted him onto the stretcher to be flown out by helicopter for emergency treatment.

She'd been trained as a first responder and knew what to do, but it's all only theory until one has their first real-life experience with such situations. This was her first time being faced with dealing with the victims of a major car crash.

She did what she was supposed to do in the way she was supposed to do it. The ranger had complimented her on her professionalism and how well she handled the situation.

As our hug continued, I felt sadness for the victims, as my heart bled for what the experience had done to our wonderfully compassionate daughter. I let the hug last for as long as she needed, hoping it would help her deal with the nightmarish scene she'd just experienced.

When she ended our hug, I was immensely grateful I'd been there when she needed a hug, and that she'd felt comfortable coming to me.

I also felt immense pride in my little girl—uh, I mean, confident and capable young woman.

I still do, and always will.

An Almost Unseen Kindness

One warm bright day after a party in a park for our grandson Thomas, while the remaining party-goers were cleaning up, I noticed out of the corner of my eye that Older Son and his wonderful wife had slipped away with a large box of pizza without saying a word to anyone.

They walked over to a homeless man who was sitting quietly and motionless on a park bench across a path from us, and perhaps fifty feet away. He had his back to us and clearly did not wish to intrude on our festivities or perhaps even be seen by us. A few words were exchanged, and they handed the box to him and quietly returned to our busy cleanup crew. When they returned, no words were spoken about what had just happened, and I doubt if anyone else had even seen what they had done. But their kindness made a proud dad and grandfather even prouder that day.

Family Nights

Picture if you will all the noise and people during rush hour in Grand Central Station, the commotion and energy of a busy dog park, the love and joy of a raucous religious revival, the laughter and entertainment of a circus, and a meal fit for a king but large enough to feed an army, and you begin to have some idea as to what it is like to be at our home most Sunday evenings.

That's because we celebrate Family Night on Sundays, and all of the above is usually generated by just my immediate family. And our dogs. Six dogs. (Our in-state adult children bring their dogs so they can play while we do.)

It's also a bit like a mini United Nations (without all the rancor, bickering, and squabbling) as my immediate family represents races from three continents.

If I ever needed a reminder as to how much abundance and love is in my life, Family Night would serve that purpose.

Family Nights are one of my favorite experiences of the week. In the midst of all the noise and activity, I often sit back and soak it all in, savoring our time together, feeling incredibly grateful to be blessed with having so many wonderful people in my life who know all my faults and love me anyway.

About the Author

Russ Towne lives with his wife in Campbell, California. They've been married since 1979. They have three adult children, four grandsons, and a granddaughter on the way. In addition to enjoying his family and friends, and his dual passions for investing and writing, Russ loves to spend time in nature, especially near rivers and streams that run through giant redwood groves and near beautiful beaches. He loves reading, watching classic movies, and tending to his small fern garden and redwood grove. Russ manages the investments of the wealth management firm he founded in 2003.

Russ has written, compiled, and published two dozen books that can be found on Amazon.com.

You'll find his Amazon Author's Page at www.amazon.com/author/russtowne.

The titles of the books he has written, compiled, published, and released include:

Nonfiction

Reflections from the Heart of a Grateful Man

From the Heart of a Grateful Man

Reflections of a Grateful Man

Slices of Life—An anthology
of the selected nonfiction stories of several writers

Honest, Honey, That's How It Happened

Fiction

Touched—Short stories and flash fiction

Palpable Imaginings—An anthology of fictional short stories
by several writers in various genres.

Poetry

Kaleidoscope

Tickletoe Tree Poetry—Humorous rhyming story poems for
children and those who are young at heart

Heart Whispers—An anthology of the selected works
of over twenty poets

Books for Young Children

The Beach That Love Built

Tickletoe Tree Poetry

A Day in the Shade of a Tickletoe Tree

The Grumpadinkles

Zach and the Toad Who Rode a Bull

Misty Zebracorn

V. G. and Dexter Dufflebee

Ki-Gra's REALLY, REALLY BIG Day!

The Duck Who Flew Upside Down

Clyde and Friends

Clyde and Hoozy Whatzadingle

Clyde and I Help a Hippo to Fly

Rusty Bear and Thomas Too

Clyde and I

Blogs

A Grateful Man (nonfiction uplifting posts): RussTowne.com

A Grateful Man's Poetry: AGratefulMansPoetry.com

Imaginings of a Grateful Man (fictional short stories): ImaginingsofaGratefulMan.com

Clyde and Friends (about writing children's stories): ClydeandFriends.com

* 9 7 8 0 6 9 2 8 0 4 1 8 6 *